Past/Imperfect:

Eric Fischl

Vernon Fisher

Laurie Simmons

This exhibition was organized with the assistance of funds from the National Endowment for the Arts, and is part of the *Viewpoints* exhibition series at Walker Art Center. Additional funding was provided by The Bush Foundation, the Dayton Hudson Foundation for Dayton's and Target Stores, the General Mills Foundation, the Honeywell Foundation, the Institute of Museum Services, The McKnight Foundation, the Minnesota State Arts Board and The Pillsbury Company Foundation.

ISBN 0935640-21-5
LC 87-050055

Travel Schedule

Walker Art Center
12 April-14 June 1987

Knight Gallery/Spirit Square Center for the Arts
Charlotte, North Carolina
11 September-7 November 1987

Contemporary Arts Center
Cincinnati, Ohio
15 January-27 February 1988

Institute of Contemporary Art University of Pennsylvania
Philadelphia, Pennsylvania
12 March-24 April 1988

Past/Imperfect:

Eric Fischl

Vernon Fisher

Laurie Simmons

Walker Art Center · Minneapolis

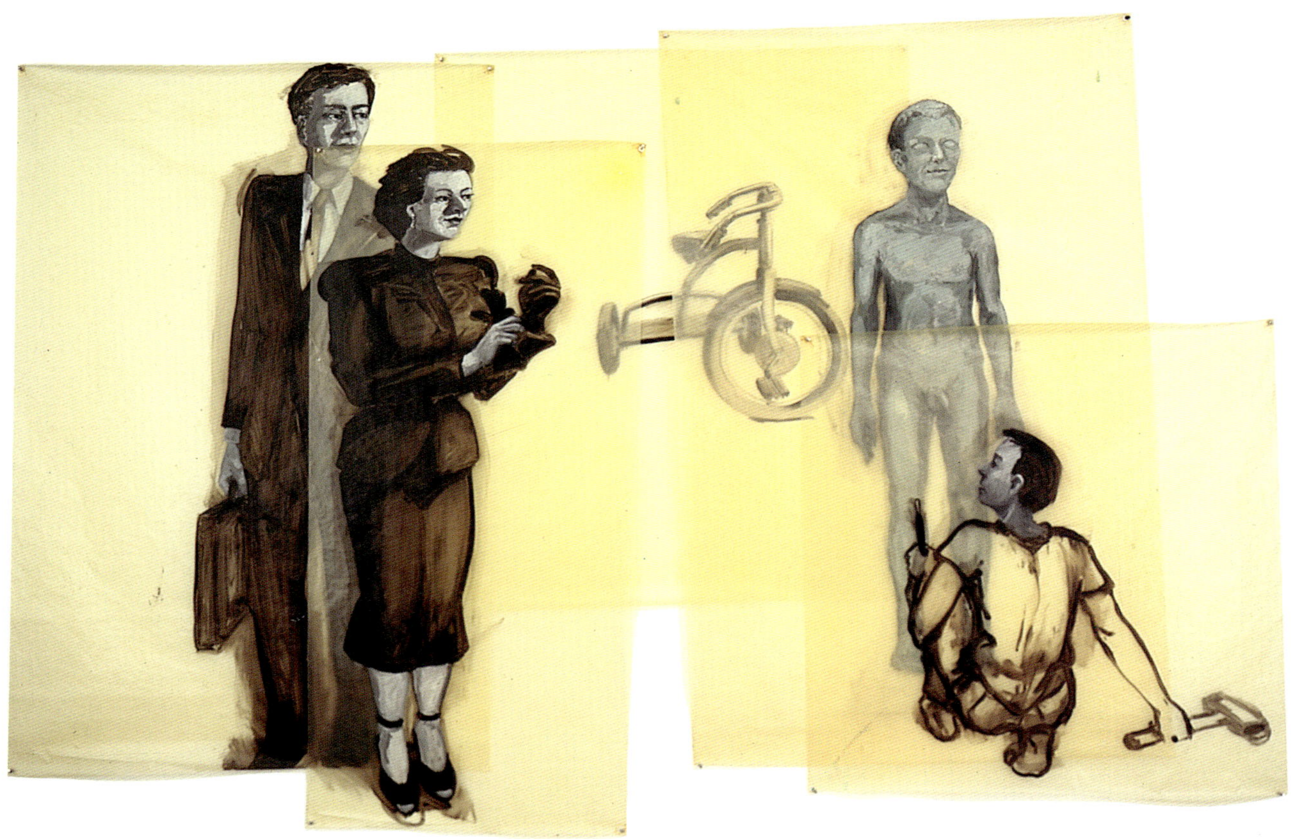

Eric Fischl
Critics   1979
oil on glassine (5 panels)
72 x 121
Collection the artist
Courtesy Mary Boone
Gallery, New York

Past/Imperfect

Marge Goldwater

The youth culture that rocks across the television screen, especially during commercial station breaks, often gives the impression that youth is as upbeat and uncomplicated as the music behind the lifestyle being touted. Eric Fischl, Vernon Fisher and Laurie Simmons are three contemporary American artists whose evocations of childhood recapture not only the proverbial good times suggested on the tube, but its darker moments as well.

The theme of childhood is hardly a new one for artists; it can be traced back to ancient times. In the post-classical world it appeared in the person of the infant Jesus. By the sixteenth century other children came to be major subjects in paintings, and they manifested a full range of adult qualities from innocence to wantonness.[1] Thus Bruegel's *Children's Games* of 1560 is an allegory of adult folly and in seventeenth-century Dutch genre painting children commented on or embodied adult concerns such as greed and sloth. The same tradition explains Chardin's *Soap Bubbles* where the boy blowing bubbles signifies the transience of life.[2]

In the late eighteenth century, after Rousseau's exaltation of innocence and imagination, childhood assumed a new, pivotal place in Western culture. Valued now for spontaneity and presumed purity, children in art were no longer stand-ins for adults in art. Instead, in paintings such as Fragonard's several scenes of happy families, these innate qualities of childhood took center stage.[3] In the nineteenth century, the reorganization of bourgeois life around the child intensified as we see in the familiar Impressionist icons of family life such as those painted by Renoir.

With the rise of modernism in the twentieth century, certain painters attempted to capture the innocence and spontaneity of youth by creating abstract work that seemed primitive in style.

Klee believed that in their drawings children represented the world without any knowledge of artistic conventions, and without regard for the way things actually looked, whereas adults tended to be consumed by a concern with form which vitiated the immediacy of the experience being conveyed. In creating a style that seemed childlike, unmindful of the accepted norms of representation, artists like Klee, Miro and Dubuffet sought to retain this immediacy. Critics regarded Klee, in particular, as an artist who had succeeded in fulfilling the definition of genius suggested by Baudelaire[4]:

> *Genius is nothing more nor less than childhood deliberately retrieved at will—a childhood now equipped for self-expression with manhood's capacities and a power of analysis which enables it to order the mass of raw material which it has involuntarily accumulated.*[5]

Several contemporary American artists today would seem to be even closer to fulfilling Baudelaire's prescription for genius, since they are engaged in a deliberate process of retrieving childhood as a direct and literal subject for their art. Neither allegorical nor abstract, their work confronts the physical and emotional experience of being a child—and of having grown up.

Jonathan Borofsky, Joel Shapiro, Scott Burton and Judith Shea are among those artists who have explored the theme of childhood, all of them at a beginning stage in their careers. With the exception of Borofsky, their approach is more abstract than narrative. The small scale of Shapiro's sculpture, especially his early toylike works such as the 1972 untitled group of four objects (p. 7) evokes a child's world. Another untitled work of the following year (p. 7) recalls parent-child relations in its abstract representation of the family unit. Shea developed a visual shorthand to project the poignancy of adolescence. In such sculptural representations of clothing as *Judy, Peggy, Kathy* (1980), three differently colored versions of the same blouse form symbolize both the teenagers' longing for peer acceptance through group conformity and, at the same time, the need for individuation. With *Child's Table and Chair* of 1978 (p. 7), Burton succinctly summarizes the innocence and aspirations of childhood. The dainty pastel colors and the reflective surfaces of the seat cushion and desk top suggest an openness and receptivity characteristic of youngsters, while the little wheels attached to

(opposite, above)
Joel Shapiro
Untitled 1972
balsa wood, bronze
bridge: 3 x 20¼ x 3
boat: 1⅝ x 11⅝ x 2⅝
coffin: 1¾ x 7⅟₁₆ x 2¾
bird: 1¾ x 3¾ x 2¾
Collection the artist

(opposite, middle)
Joel Shapiro
Untitled 1973
oil on wood and masonite
3 units, left to right:
5 x 3½; 8 x 8; 5½ x 5½
Collection Claire Mahot
Courtesy Paula Cooper
Gallery, New York

(opposite, below)
Scott Burton
Child's Table and Chair
1978
lacquered wood and polished stainless steel with brass casters; leather and foam cushion
table: 21 x 22 x 17
chair: 27 x 2 x 12
Collection Charles and Doris Saatchi, London

both the chair and desk legs imply a freedom and mobility that is seldom the condition of adulthood.

Borofsky's painting and sculpture is essentially narrative and specific. His 1972 *Mom, I Lost the Election* (p. 8) recounts, through its imagery and somewhat childlike rendering, the emotions of the schoolboy who, with head downcast, is being picked up by his mother after classes. Borofsky chronicles his artistic coming of age in *Age Piece* (p. 8), an ongoing work, begun in 1972, which includes a selection of the paintings and sculpture he has made since the age of eight.

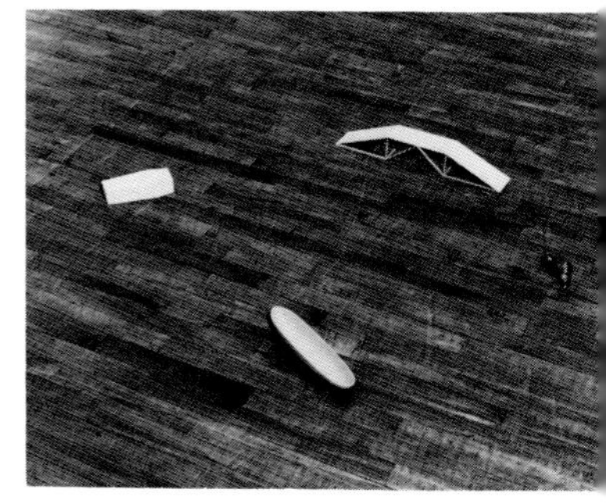

The three artists whose work is represented in this exhibition, Eric Fischl, Vernon Fisher and Laurie Simmons, also interpret childhood through narrative means, as mentioned earlier. Simmons's work is concerned with the fundamental questions of identity that a child confronts; she uses dolls as surrogates to act out this search for self-definition. Typically she has focused on females and alluded to the particular problems young girls face in modern society in a manner that is quite deliberately political rather than personal. Fischl, too, is preoccupied with the ways in which youngsters—in his work, male—start to define themselves. Over the years he has expanded his cast of characters to include those beyond the immediate family and moved into less personal territory. As a result, he has widened the range of emotions and environments he portrays. Unlike Simmons and Fischl, whose imagery is presented from the child's vantage point, Fisher's narratives are seen from the comfortable distance of adulthood. In his work childhood has already been analyzed and resolved. Although this resolution offers cause for optimism, we see the past Fisher portrays—like those of Simmons and Fischl—is often imperfect.

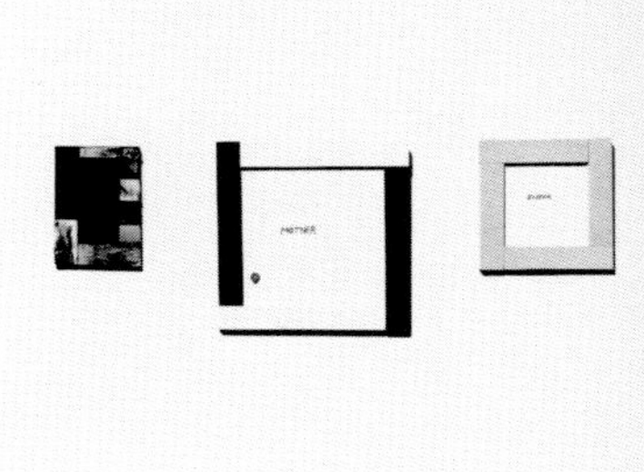

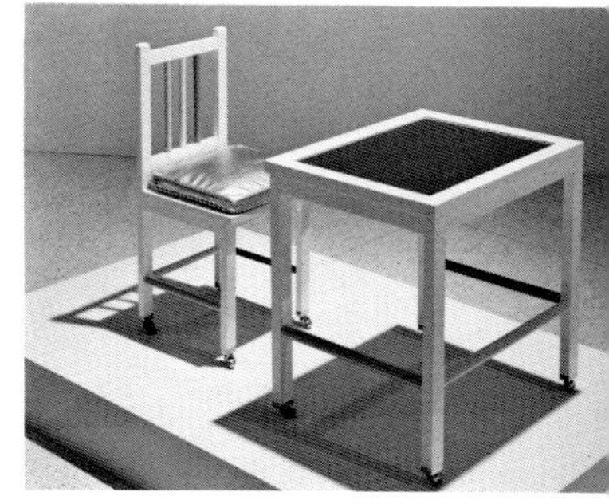

Initially Fischl combined words and images in his paintings, creating a narrative series about a fisher family in Nova Scotia, where he was teaching in the early seventies. When a friend challenged him to make paintings that more directly evoked his own experience, he began portraying middle-class America, but with an autobiographical cast. "None of my paintings," he has remarked, "is strictly autobiographical, but the tone of the work has everything to do with my childhood."[6]

Fischl's paintings are in a sense exorcistic. They allow him to recreate a situation from the past in order to finally master it.

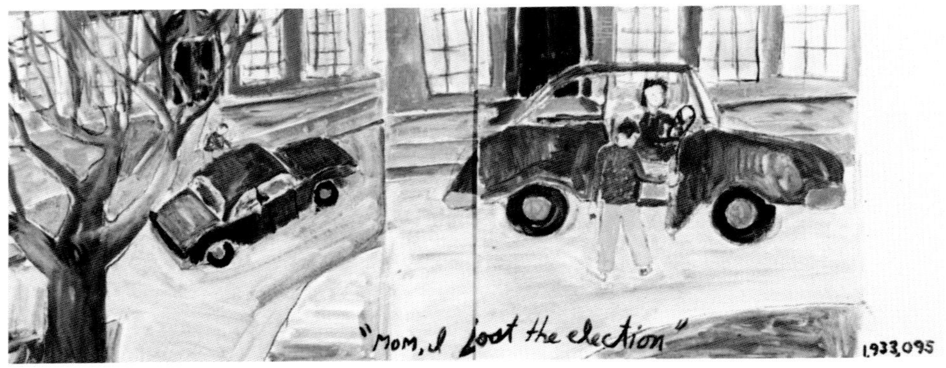

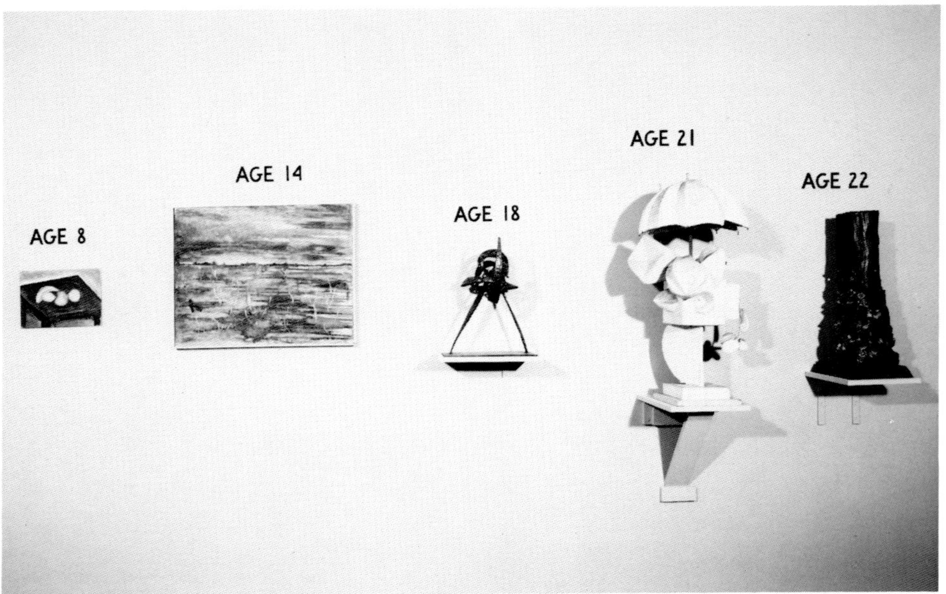

The multipartite structure of so many of them, in particular the layered works on glassine, suggests the possibility of rearranging the figures and objects until the most desirable result is achieved.[7] The representation of individuals on separate sheets of paper also implies their isolation from one another, while the unfinished character of the figures in this group of works reinforces the sense of irresolution in their interrelationships. The inherently fragile nature of the glassine also speaks of vulnerability.

Through these formal means, no less than through the suggested narratives, Fischl is trying to gain control of an imperfect past by creating a body of work about the often difficult experience

8

of coming of age in America—from the perspective of youth. This perspective is always clear from the narrative, but sometimes it is visually emphasized as well. In *Sleepwalker* (p. 9) the young boy occupies the center of the canvas, confronted, as we are, by the symbolic adult presence in the form of two lawn chairs. The direct gaze of the awkward adolescent in the foreground draws us into *Funeral*, presumably about the death of the artist's mother. In *Bad Boy* as well we enter the work looking over the boy's shoulder and thus share his vantage point.

The tales Fischl tells depart from tradition not only because

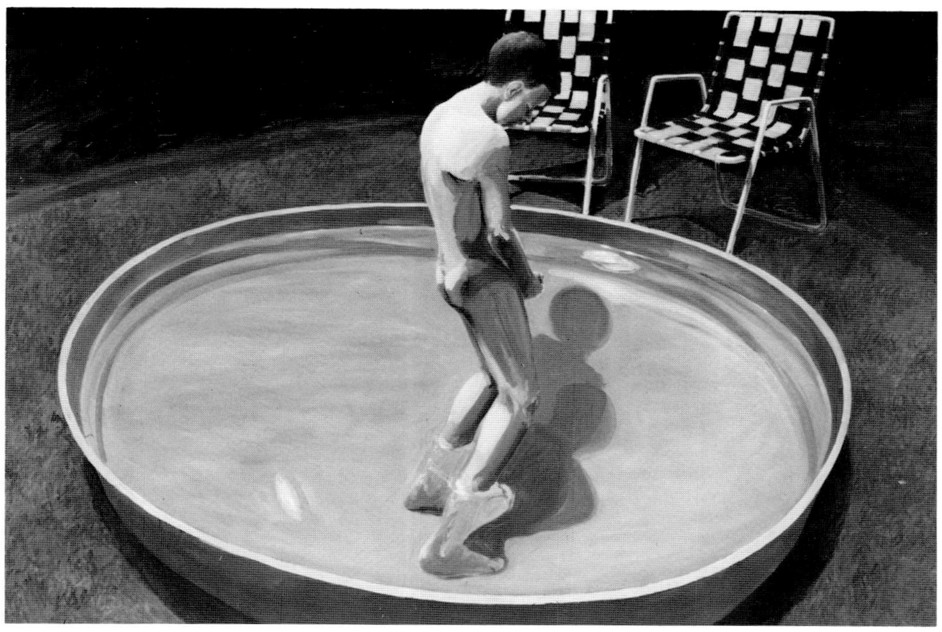

they speak with the child's voice, but also because their primary concern is to illuminate the conditions of childhood itself rather than to serve as a metaphor for the world of adults. In works such as *Horse and Rider* (p. 12) and *Slumber Party*, where the child stands alone or plays with other children, the children represent only themselves and the narrative is primarily concerned with their developing sense of sexuality and at times, their loss of innocence, as in *Sleepwalker*. While works such as *Squirt, The Old Man's Boat and the Old Man's Dog*, and numerous others have elements both of eroticism and perversion, the reference is never to adult immorality. Rather, children are full-fledged players with indepen-

Eric Fischl
Sleepwalker 1979
oil on canvas
72 x 108
Collection Edward R.
Downe, Jr.
Courtesy Mary Boone
Gallery, New York

dent voices whose actions and desires carry the same weight as those of their elders. Both versions of *Best Western* (p. 13) featuring a youngster highlighted against a dark and foreboding background, illustrate the darker side of children's behavior. The boy's total absorption with his toy Indians is typical of a child. According to the artist, the scene of the boy torturing these figures brought forth numerous confessions from friends of similar episodes in their own childhoods.[8]

This also holds true in Fischl's many paintings about family relations, which provide a series of unique variations on the artistic tradition of parent and child portraiture. The oil on glassine painting *Mother and Son at Table* (p. 11) replaces the mother's sweet glow with an air of detachment while the son's face expresses pent-up anger. *Dancing Daughter, Father and Son Sleeping, Daddy's Girl* and *Birthday Party* (p. 11) openly defy tradition, presenting disturbing and unforgettable images that suggest unnatural relations between parents and children in paintings charged with the sexual tension that specifically defines Fischl's work.

Relations among siblings also come within Fischl's purview, and they are hardly of the Dick and Jane variety. In *Horse and Rider* the brother coolly keeps his sister on a tight rein in a rather perverse form of child's play. The sister—a child's body with a woman's head—is perched angrily on her tricycle as she pulls her brother along on a rolling chair. While the two naked figures in *Sisters*, a later work, are not combative, there is still an air of Balthusian malevolence hanging over this scene of two young women in a bathroom, one of them poised over a bidet, the other seemingly indifferent to her surroundings.

(opposite, above)
Eric Fischl
Birthday Party   1980
oil on glassine (4 panels)
69 x 76
Collection the artist
Courtesy Mary Boone
Gallery, New York

(opposite, below)
Eric Fischl
*Mother and Son at
Table*   1978
oil on glassine (5 panels)
72 x 121
Collection the artist
Courtesy Mary Boone
Gallery, New York

Unlike Fischl, who describes childhood with a vocabulary of realism in the tradition of Edward Hopper, Laurie Simmons explores some of the same territory through the medium of photography. And in her work, the medium itself, with its tendency to miniaturize, becomes part of the commentary. Standing outside the realm of traditional photography, Simmons records a world of artistic invention rather than natural circumstance, a choice underscored in her early work by vivid but highly artificial color and in subsequent series by the conflicting scales of figure and ground.

In 1977 Simmons began constructing and photographing miniature tableaux (p. 15), using dolls and dollhouse furniture as

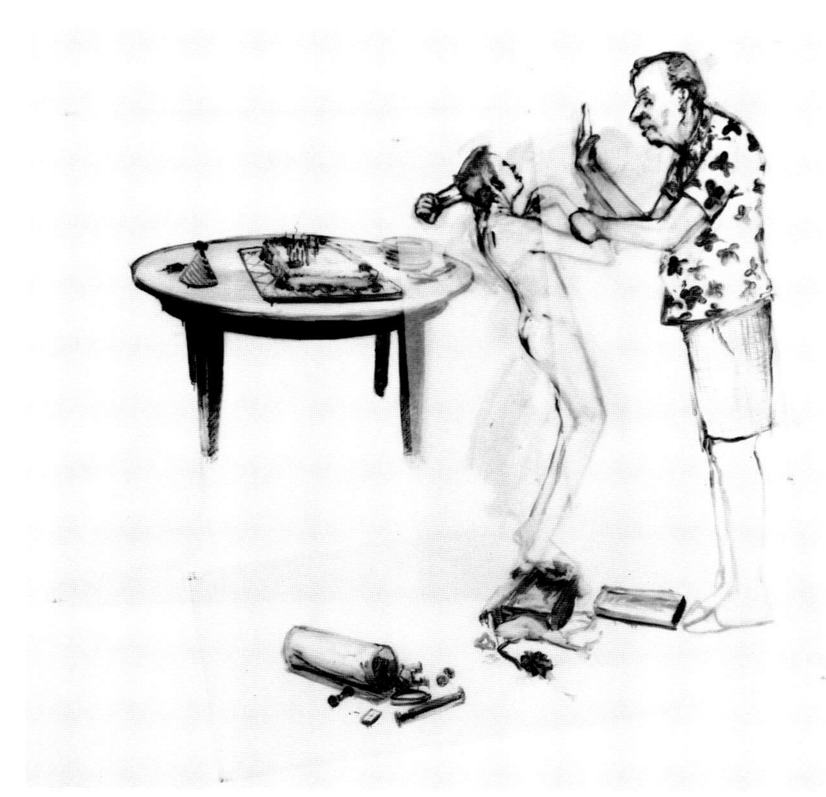

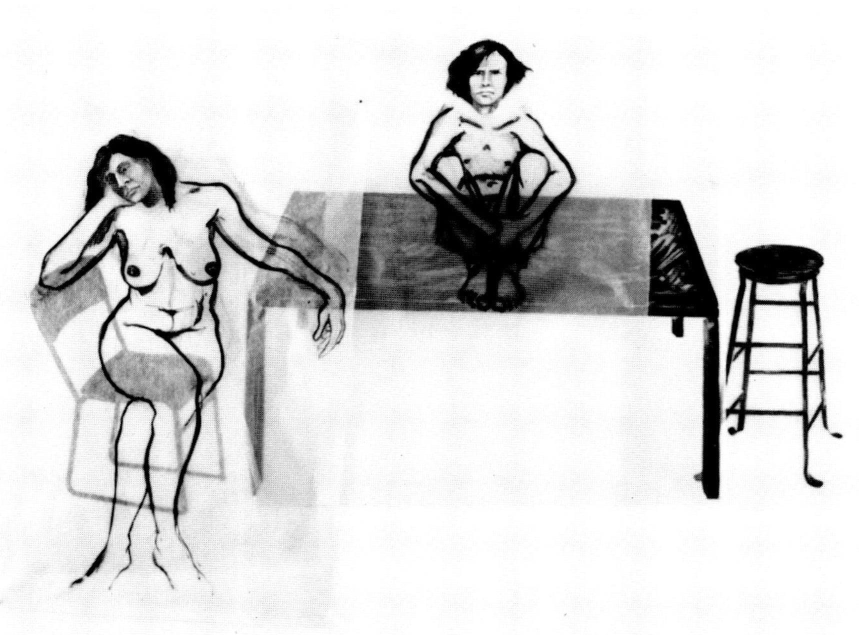

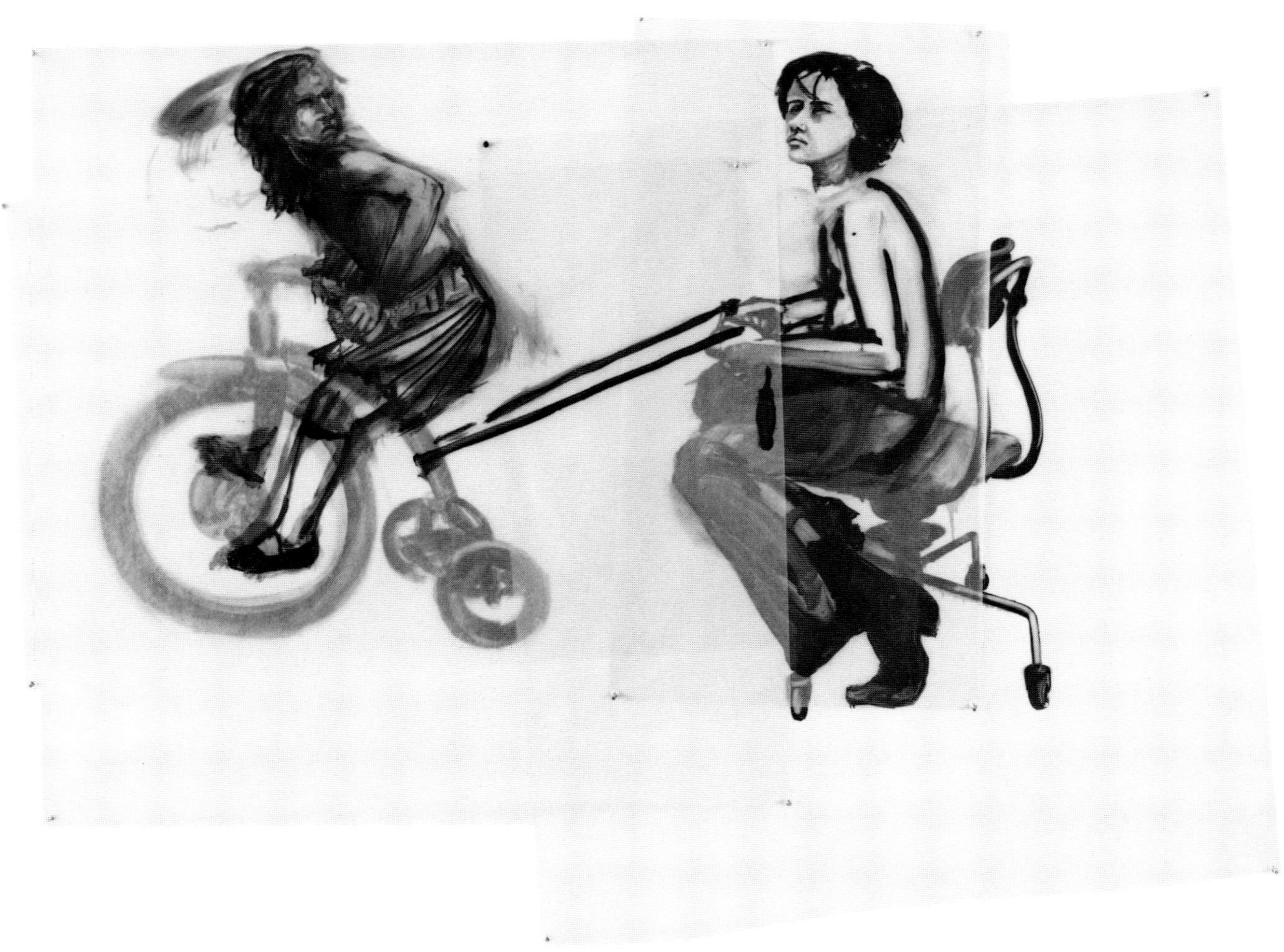

Eric Fischl
Horse and Rider   1979
oil on glassine (4 panels)
60 x 79
Collection the artist
Courtesy Mary Boone
Gallery, New York

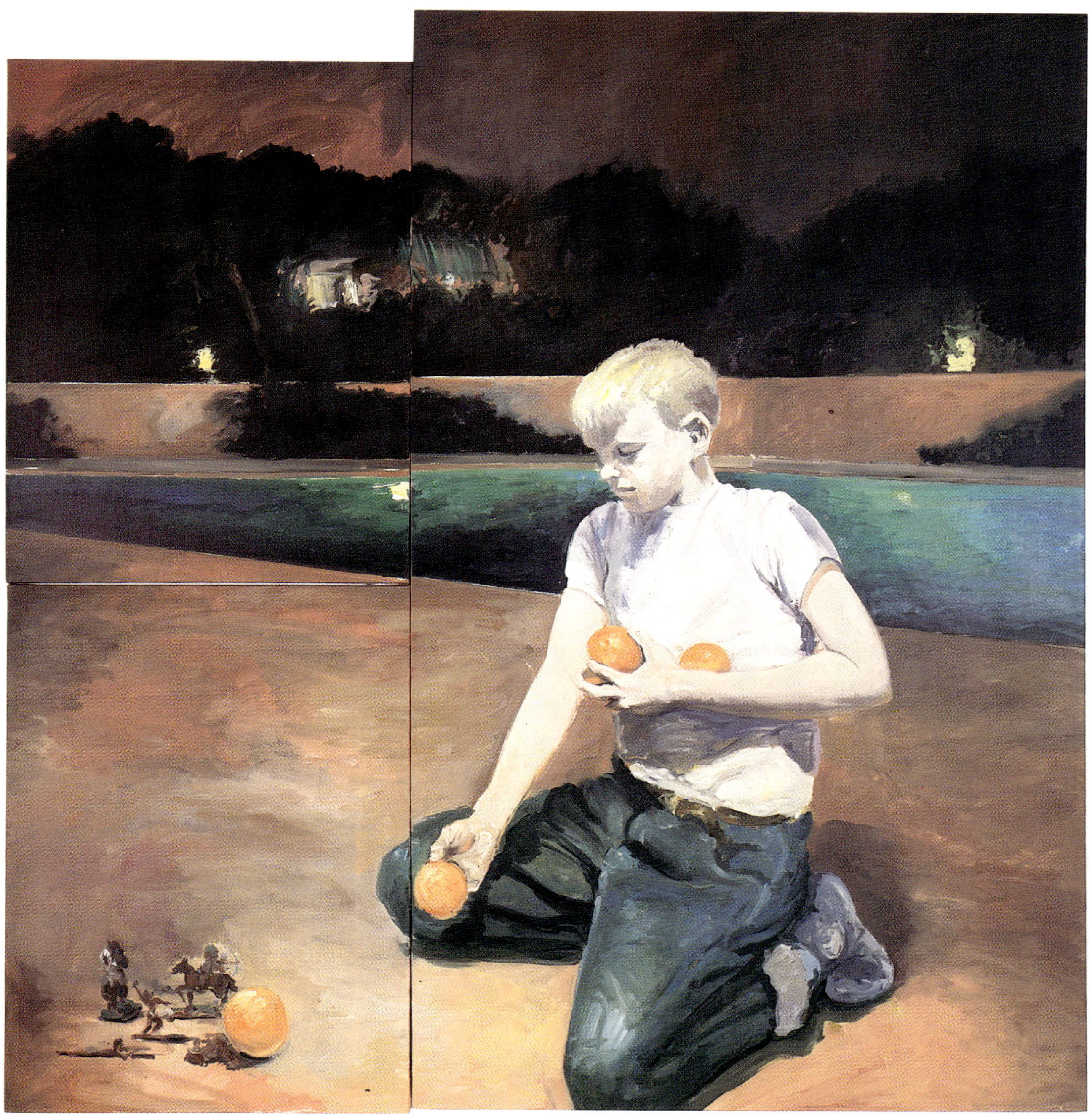

Eric Fischl
Best Western
(first version)   1983
oil on canvas (3 panels)
84 x 80
Collection the artist
Courtesy Mary Boone
Gallery, New York

stand-in players and props to make a statement about growing up and being grown up. The tableaux do not include children; they present instead a miniature staged vision of what children see and remember. And if the scale of these works evokes childhood pastimes, it also provides a situation in which Simmons can exercise the kind of total control that children themselves enjoy when playing with dolls, but which eludes them in real-life situations. As with Fischl's work, the series represents an attempt to restage events so as to get them right. One perceives these photographs as though looking through a peephole or viewfinder; they set up a longing to be in a place which one can no longer enter—as if returning to one's childhood home only to find that one has outgrown it; the doors are too small and the bed is too short.

At the same time that these photographs deftly suggest a child's vision and experience of the world, they also articulate certain adult concerns—in the visual language of the child. Unlike the art of the past, in which children symbolically represented the adult world, here we are given the child's perception of adulthood, complete with mother-dolls. But in Simmons's tableaux, adult perceptions inform the child's vision: what the child remembers seeing, the adult understands. The claustrophobic feeling of Simmons's interiors and the often aggressive quality of the color present a jaundiced view of the life of the fifties housewife, as in *New Bathroom/Woman Standing* (p. 15), with its powder-blue paradise of a bathroom—and a woman scrubbing to keep it that way. Simmons succeeds in giving us the viewpoints of young and old simultaneously in these formally compelling photographs.

After completing the Dollhouse series, Simmons worked for a time with live models, photographing them in color under water. But she found the process in this Swimmer series cumbersome and went back to the dolls, which she photographed as she randomly dropped them in the shallow end of a swimming pool. The resulting series, Family Collision (p. 16-17), includes approximately sixteen black-and-white photographs, sixteen color photographs, and a diptych that combines one of each. In contrast to the lyrical and seductive Swimmers, this group of works is rather bleak. The black-and-white photographs appear to be ghost images of the earlier Swimmer series, a faded memory of its colorful figures. The photographs in the Family Collision series that feature a configuration of family members floating independently under water imply communication problems of a magnitude seen in Fischl's

(opposite, above)
Laurie Simmons
New Bathroom/Woman Standing 1978/87
color photograph
40 x 50
Courtesy Metro Pictures, New York

(opposite, below)
Laurie Simmons
Woman/Purple Dress/Kitchen 1978/87
color photograph
40 x 50
Collection Walker Art Center Jerome Foundation Purchase Fund For Emerging Artists

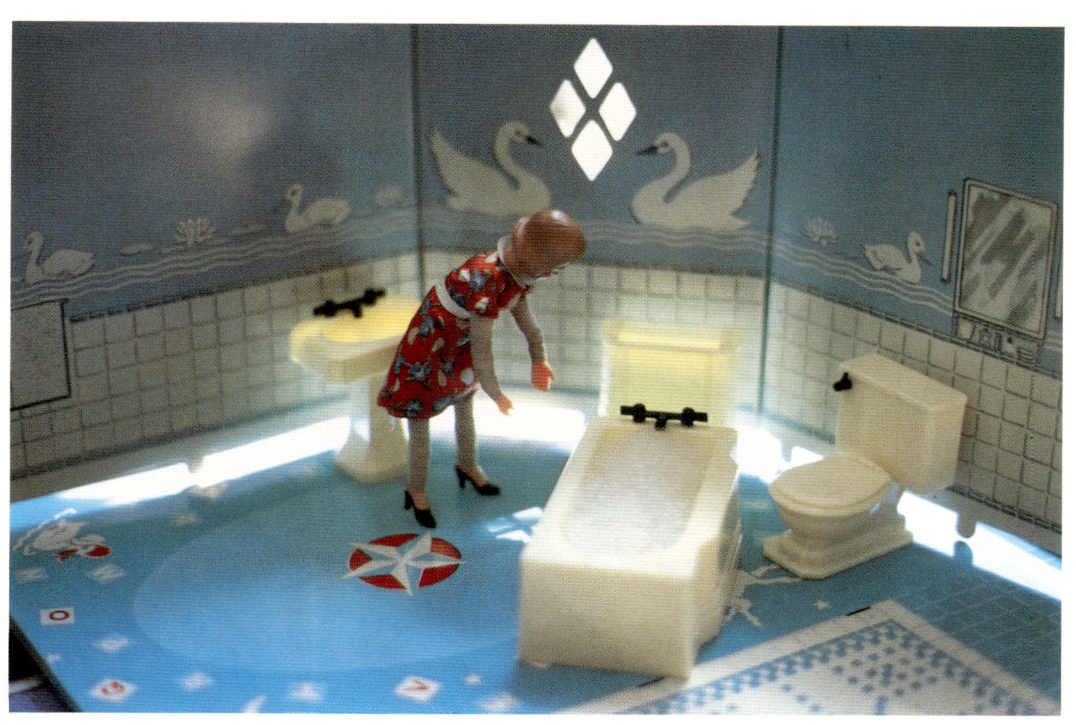

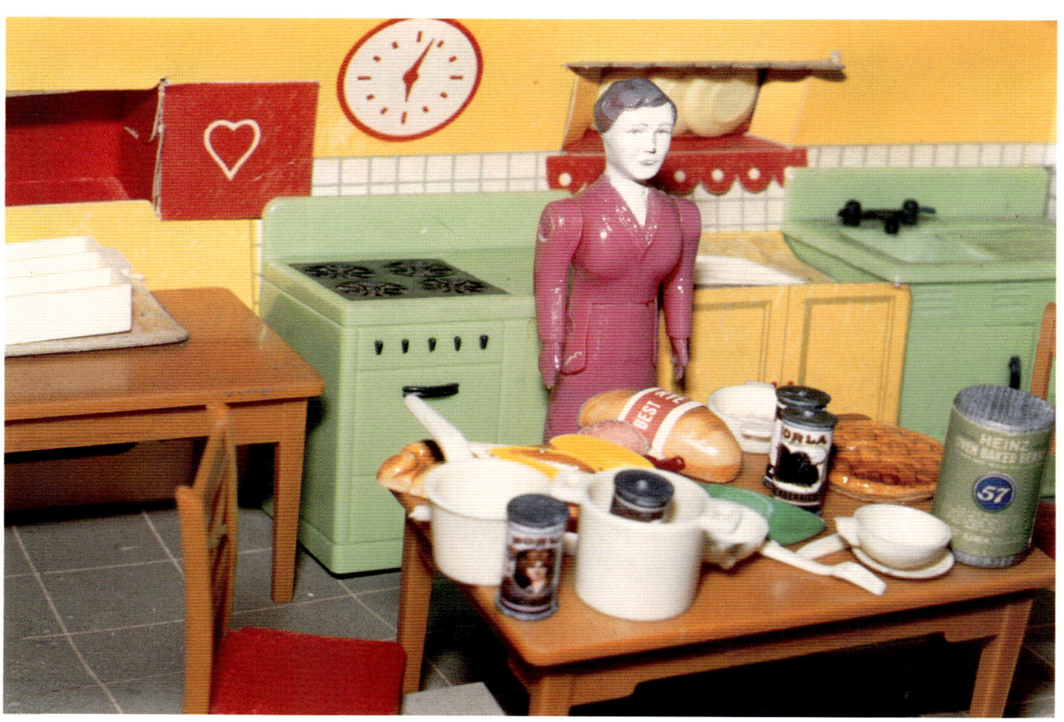
BEST
ORLA
HEINZ
OVEN BAKED BEANS
57

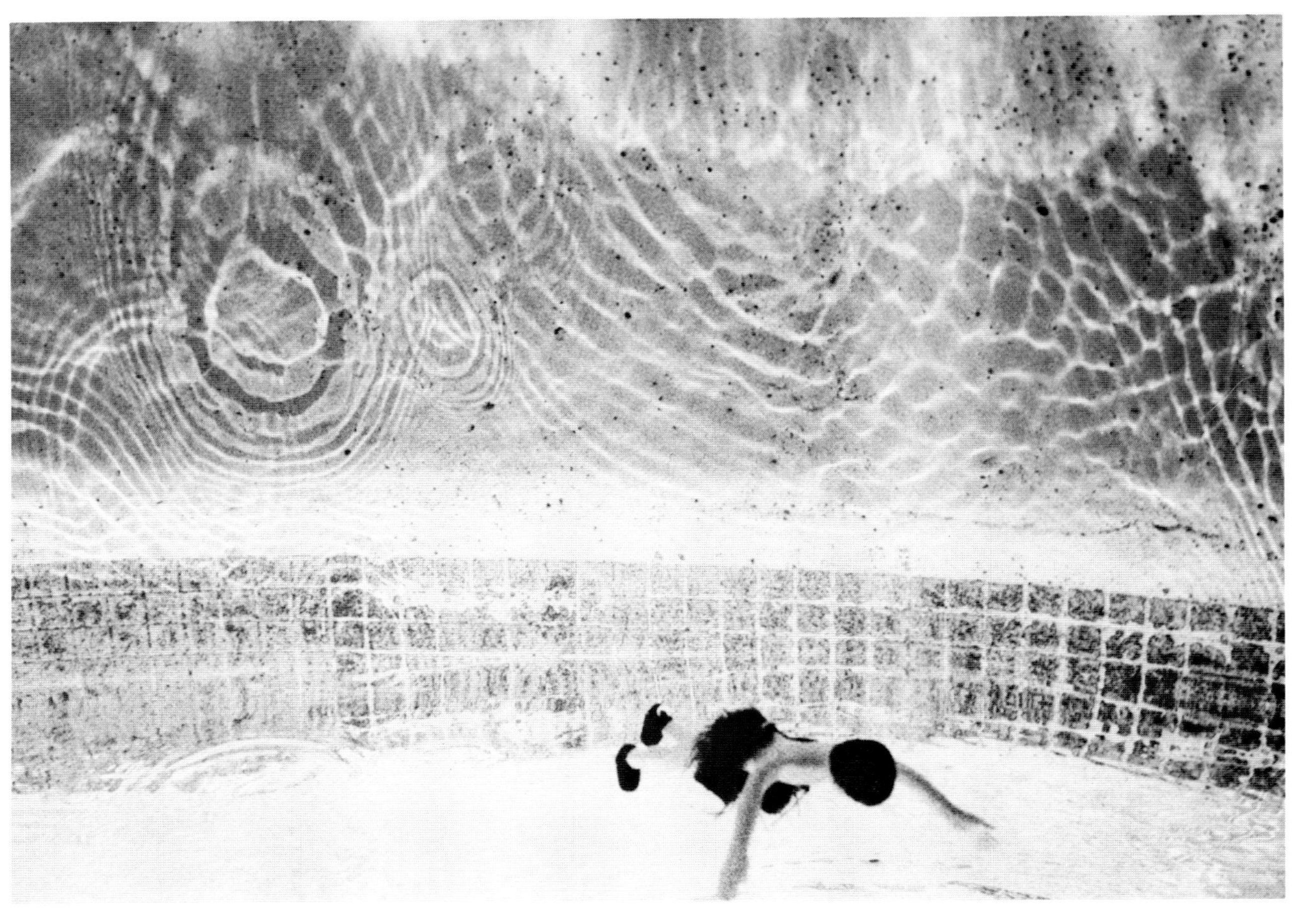

scenarios, where individuals are physically isolated on separate sheets of glassine. The predicament of Simmons's figures is highly ambiguous: one is not sure whether they are casting about for an identity in uncharted seas, as their tiny bodies in vast surroundings suggest, or drowning. If the Dollhouse series could be characterized as claustrophobic, these newer works have a deathlike edge to them, hinting at what psychiatrists know to be the commonplace childhood obsession with death and morbidity.

The Ventriloquism series (p. 18), Simmons's newest body of work, uses a different set of surrogates: live models (hired ventriloquists) with dummies on their knees. Introducing male figures for the first time, she presents both live model and boy figure (the

(above and opposite)
Laurie Simmons
Untitled (from Family
Collison series)   1981
black-and-white photographs
16 x 20 each
Collection Caroll Dunham

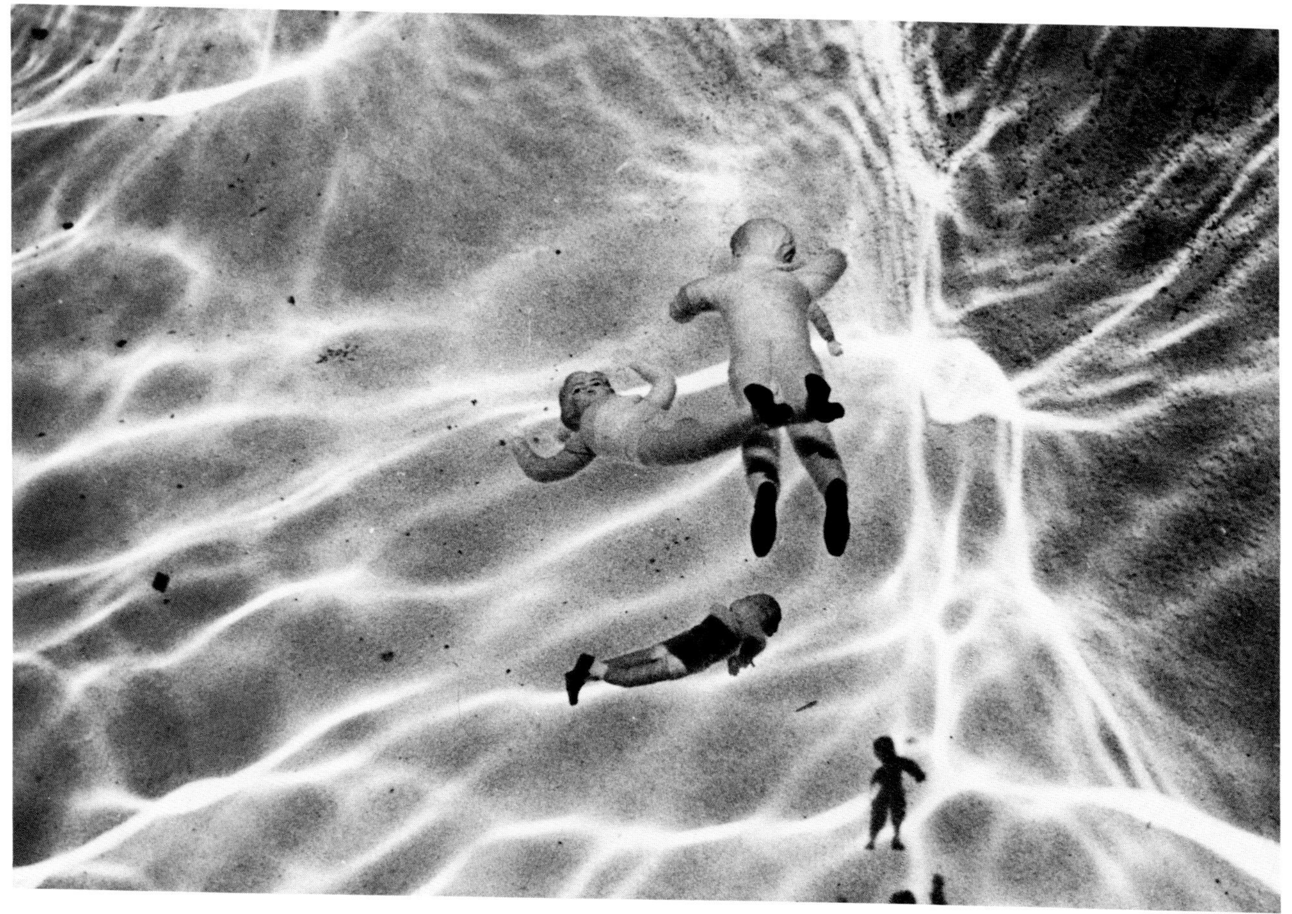

professional's term for a dummy) against her familiar format of a projected backdrop—an interior or landscape, a borrowed image usually taken from a magazine, book or vintage postcard.

The use of surrogates is not the only familiar element. In this series-in-progress, Simmons comments once again on the nature of photography, pointing to the confusion it presents between the real and the contrived. She also returns to the issue of control addressed in the Dollhouse series. There the small scale enabled her to manipulate the environment she was photographing to gain total dominance. In the Ventriloquism series, the idea of domination is directly confronted. The infantilization of the boy figure, its complete dependency on the ventriloquist for animation, becomes

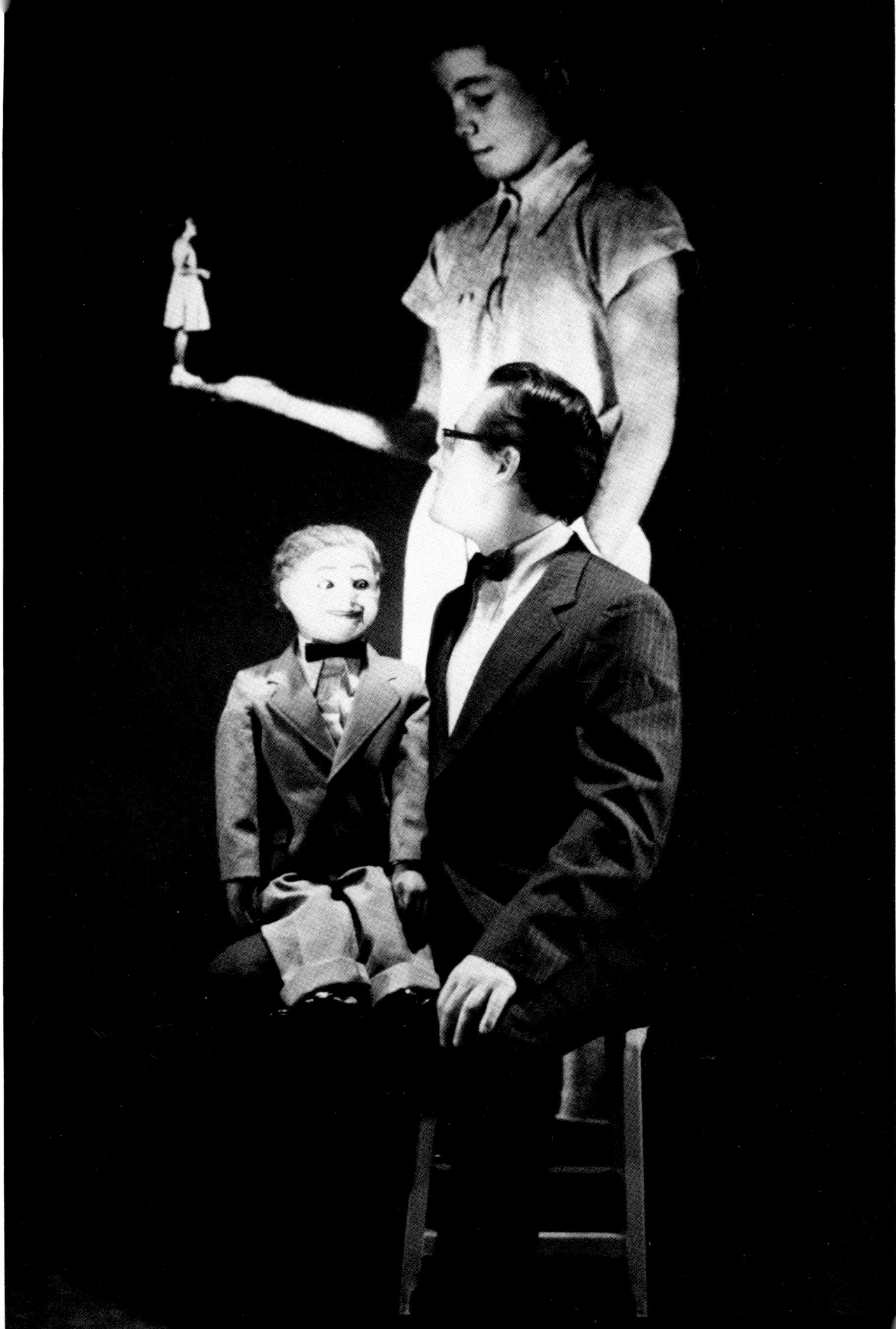

a metaphor for one type of parent-child relationship and for any situation in which one person is dominated by another.

The juxtaposition of the figure against the projected image in the Ventriloquism series largely avoids the important paradox to be found in many of Simmons's other photographs. As in Fischl's work, her photographs represent an attempt to restage certain episodes, to manage them better the second time around. And yet the inevitable consequence of shooting doll-size objects against a real-life situation, be it a swimming pool or the Pyramids, as in her more recent Tourism series, means, of course, that the elements will forever be irreconcilable. This method of construction denies the possibility of ever "getting things right." The figures are consigned to a life of discomfort in their respective environments.

Vernon Fisher's works often have a domestic context and his many paintings relating to childhood filter past episodes through an adult lens, suggesting both the continuing need to reexamine and unravel these experiences and the ways in which they have an abiding influence on one's life. Fisher combines images and texts to create multilayered works that imply the passage of time. In some cases, the text is laid directly on the image; in others, it may appear in a panel by itself. He frequently constructs his paintings in several parts, occasionally incorporating sculptural objects. These objects introduce a foil, what Fisher describes as the "reality factor."[9] They constitute a physical presence that represents the here and now. Meanwhile, the verbal narrative conveys an earlier time and the painted image offers an illusory "reality." By implying a long time span, Fisher assures us we do survive childhood experiences and eventually integrate them into our adult lives.

Children at play is Fisher's theme, but unlike the artistic tradition exemplified by Bruegel, Fisher emphasizes what the play experience represented to the child and how the adult draws upon that experience. His works generally develop from a story—for example, an expanded version of a fragment of conversation he has overheard or an experience at the supermarket. He then selects images from the stockpile of slides he has assembled over the years and sorted by subject: landscapes, marine diagrams, physics diagrams, war, personal, etc. When he has finally arrived at the right combination—or juxtaposition—of images and text, he projects the slides onto the canvas and begins to paint. He is careful not

Laurie Simmons
Untitled (from Ventriloquism series) 1987
photogravure
33½ x 26⅝
Courtesy Editions Ilene Kurtz

19

to illustrate the text with images; rather, text and image illuminate each other by analogy, providing parallel stories. In Fisher's words, "I use fiction the way other people use blue."[10]

Tarzan's Adventure (p. 23) expresses the feelings aroused by watching Tarzan movies on television both as a child and as an adult. The text's narrator remarks that as he watches the movie now he is aware of the artifice of the production, which he did not see as a child. Nevertheless, he is still affected by the fakery and immediately transported to "the innocent, balmy days of child-hood," when the jungle scenes looked real instead of like Hollywood backdrops. The loss of innocence described here is a more integrated experience than that offered in Fischl's work, because it represents a later consideration of loss. Like Simmons, Fisher on occasion presents both adult and child concerns simultaneously, but he differs both from Simmons and Fischl in locating the childhood experiences he recounts in the past. Perhaps most important in *Tarzan's Adventure* is the sense of closed off time and space, a feeling that also characterizes Simmons's work. She creates it by miniaturizing the space, by making it too large for an adult to enter; Fisher conveys the feeling through the window construction and the dense trellis, overgrown with vines (p. 21, 23). The window, which suggests an opening into the past, faces a blank wall, while the vines are impenetrable.

The text of *When I Was a Kid* (p. 25) shares with *Tarzan's Adventure* the vantage point of adulthood. Reflecting back on the Easter egg hunt, the grown-up Fisher realizes that there was a system for hiding the eggs, which the child remained ignorant of. Breaking the code—here, figuring out that the eggs are always hidden by an object, in *Tarzan's Adventure*, perceiving the fakery of the setting—is a persistent theme in Fisher's work; and it signifies the end of innocence. This idea is also highlighted in the grid structure at the right of *When I Was a Kid*, within which eggs are visibly "hidden." The Erector set toys pictured in the text panel reinforce the idea of child's play. The nostalgic element of the old-fashioned fan, with an egg lying at its base, also refers back to the text. The egg is painted the same color as the fan, a bit of camouflage to recall the child's incomprehension of the system of hiding eggs near objects.

Boy Throwing Airplane (p. 28), whose text describes a young boy distracted from his reading lessons by the lure of faraway places, is also about breaking a code. Only with great difficulty

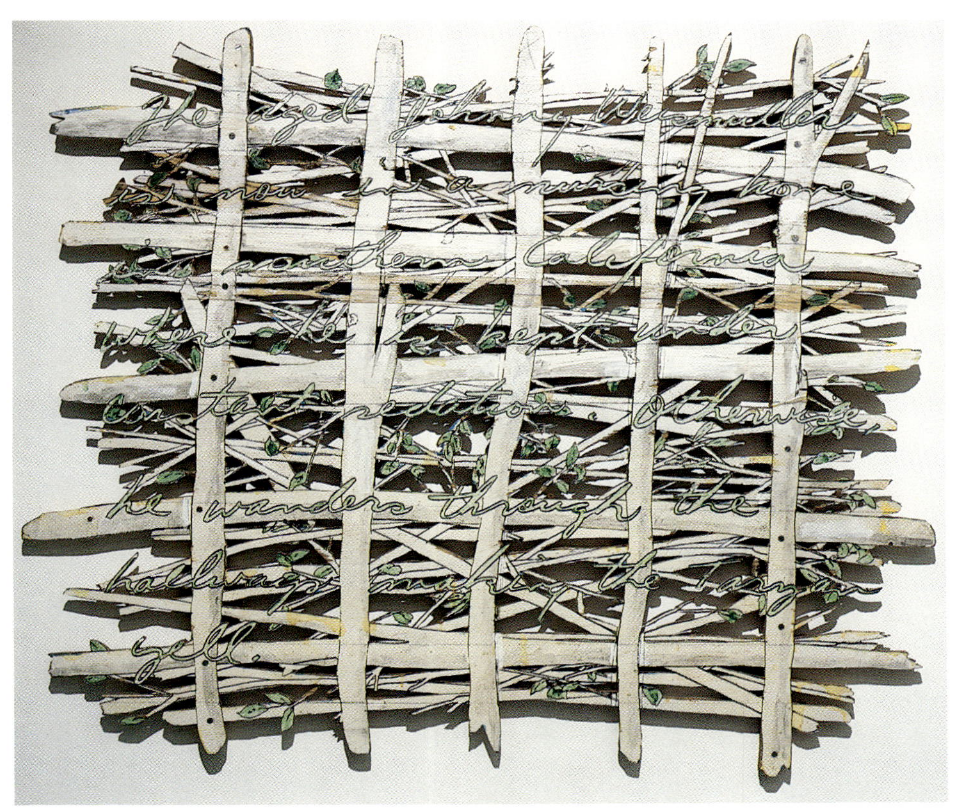

does one decipher the painting's text, which is concealed by a background resembling both a marbelized school notebook and the "black and foamy waves" to which the text alludes. Eventually we discover from the text that the boy won't be able to go to the movies unless he can improve his reading. And the image of the boy playing with a toy airplane suggests that his prospects are not good. Fisher encourages empathy with the youth's plight by engaging the viewer in a similar struggle, one which recalls the intensity and confusion of childhood. The text concerning the radio broadcast about the Korean War locates the work within a narrow time frame, but implicitly contrasts the boy's small personal world with international political realities. In this context, Fisher adds an ironic touch: the broadcaster is reporting General MacArthur's assurance that China will not intervene in the war. The foolishness of an adult authority figure is thus set against the child's more readily excusable lapse in judgment.

Vernon Fisher
Tarzan's Adventure
(detail)   1980
acrylic on wood, graphite,
plexiglas, paint on wall
48 x 174
Collection Laura L. Carpenter

Vernon Fisher
Tarzan's Adventure

It is Saturday afternoon again, and I am watching another Tarzan movie on T.V. There has been one each Saturday for six Saturdays in a row and I have seen each one. This one is about Tarzan trying to save the sacred elephant burial ground from greedy ivory hunters. Just now, Tarzan has walked into the hunter's camp. Music is coming from a box in the foreground. It is his first experience with a photograph. He pulls his knife.

A lot of what seemed so real to me as a child, now looks clumsy and obvious. The jungle looks fake, shot on a Hollywood backlot, and I can always tell when they're using back projection for the dangerous scenes. Yet, despite the artifice, I'm still drawn to them. It's as though they constitute for me a kind of primary reality, and seeing them now, thirty years later, is like experiencing again the innocent, balmy days of childhood.

The white hunters have mortally wounded an elephant and are following it, hoping it will lead them to the elephants' graveyard. In the jungle, they stumble upon a doll-like figure pinned to a tree. They stare at the tiny figure in astonishment. One mutters worriedly, "This used to be a full grown man."

Later, in the camp, everyone is sitting close to the fire. Deep in the jungle, the Ju Jus are beating their hollow drums. The rhythm is incessant, maddening. Everyone is checking his rifle and exchanging anxious looks. After a while, the little memsaib clasps her hands to her ears and screams, "Those horrible drums, I can't stand it anymore." Instantly, they stop. It becomes quiet. Firelight flickers across motionless figures.

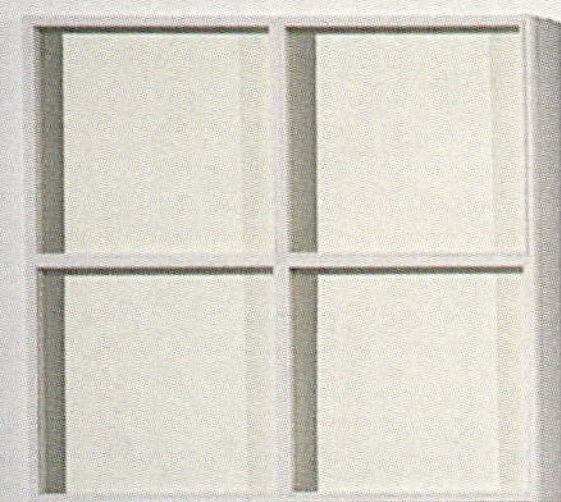

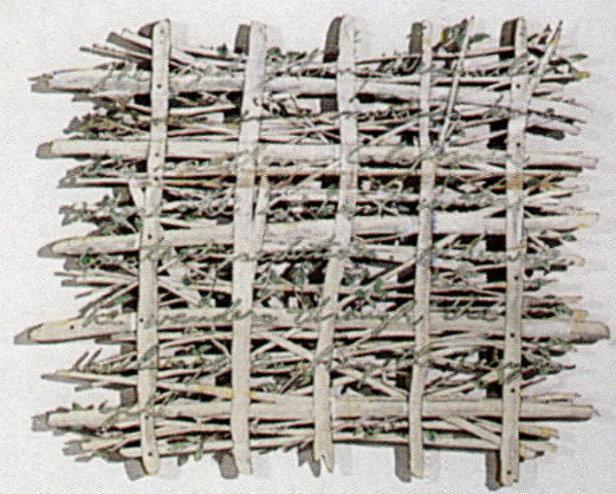

Vernon Fisher
Tarzan's Adventure   1980
acrylic on wood, graphite,
plexiglas, paint on wall
(3 units)
48 x 174
Collection Laura L. Carpenter

Vernon Fisher
When I Was a Kid

When I was a kid I was never any good
at finding Easter eggs. At the class
Easter egg hunt, everyone would run
yelling and screaming after the eggs,
finding them right and left until their
baskets practically ran over, while I
stumbled around never finding any
unless it was one that had been
stepped on. It never occurred to me
that in a big grassy field the eggs
weren't just scattered at random.
Later I discovered that because we
were SUPPOSED to find them, they
were always placed next to other
objects: the bases of trees, fence posts,
water faucets, etc. I know that now,
but back then, I was unable to break
the code.

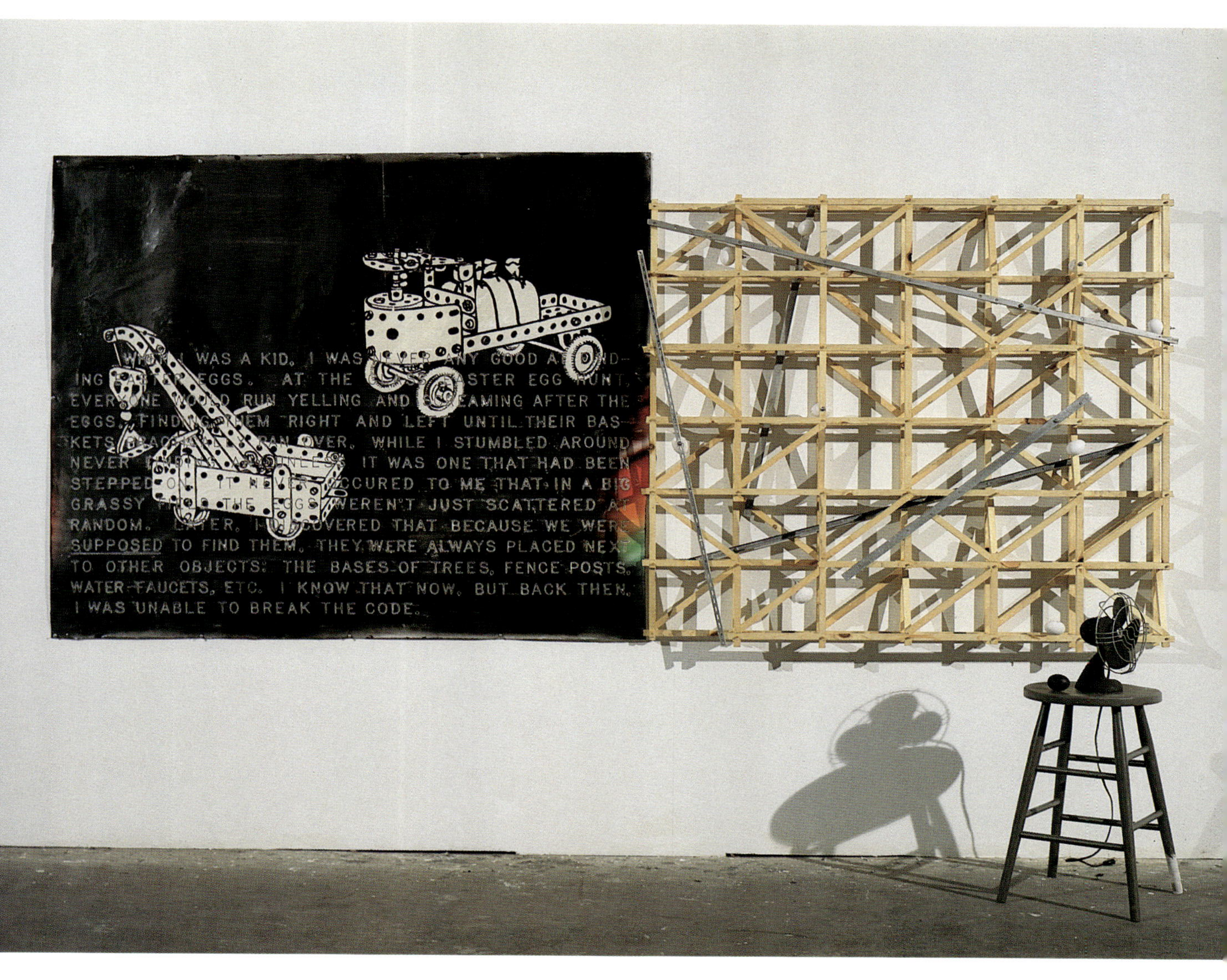

Vernon Fisher
When I Was a Kid   1983
eggs, plaster, wood, fan,
acrylic on paper, metal
60½ x 131 x 4¾
35 x 15 x 15 (fan on stool)
Collection Arthur and Carol
Goldberg, New York

One little girl never brought anything to sharing time. Other children might bring an authentic Indian headdress acquired on a vacation in Arizona, or a civil war sword handed down from great granddad, but whenever the teacher asked: "Dori, do you have anything to share with us today?" she only stared at the top of her desk and shook her head firmly from side to side.

Then one day, long after her turn had mercifully disappeared, Dori abruptly left her seat and walked to the front of the class. With everyone's startled attention she began: "Today on the way to school I found something that I want to share." She held her arm stiffly out in front of her and began slowly dropping tiny pieces of shredded kleenex. "See?" she said. "Snow."

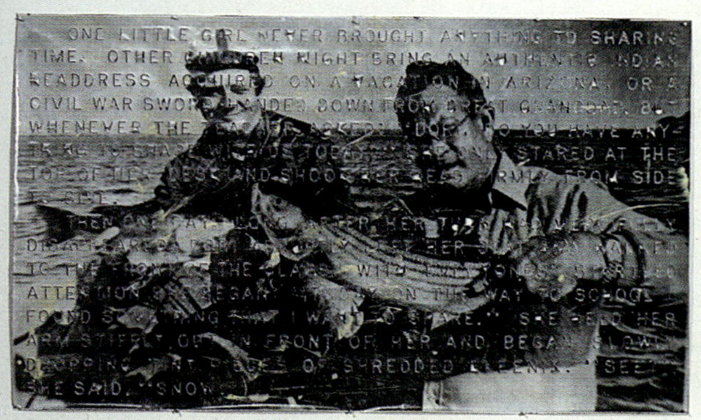

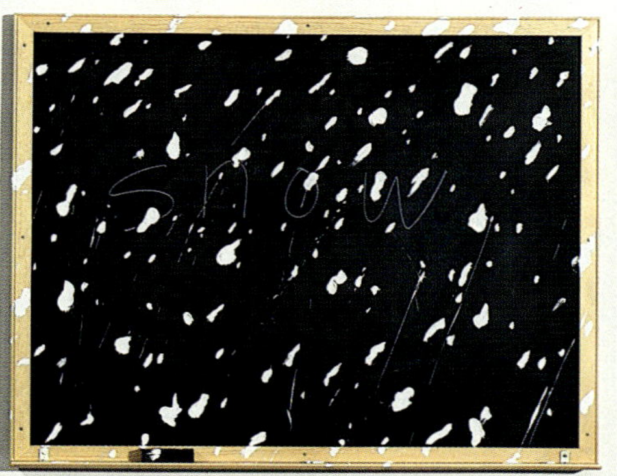

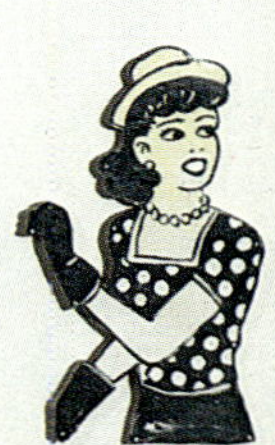

Vernon Fisher
Show and Tell   1981
photograph, oil on wood,
blackboard
60 x 174
Courtesy Barbara Gladstone
Gallery, New York

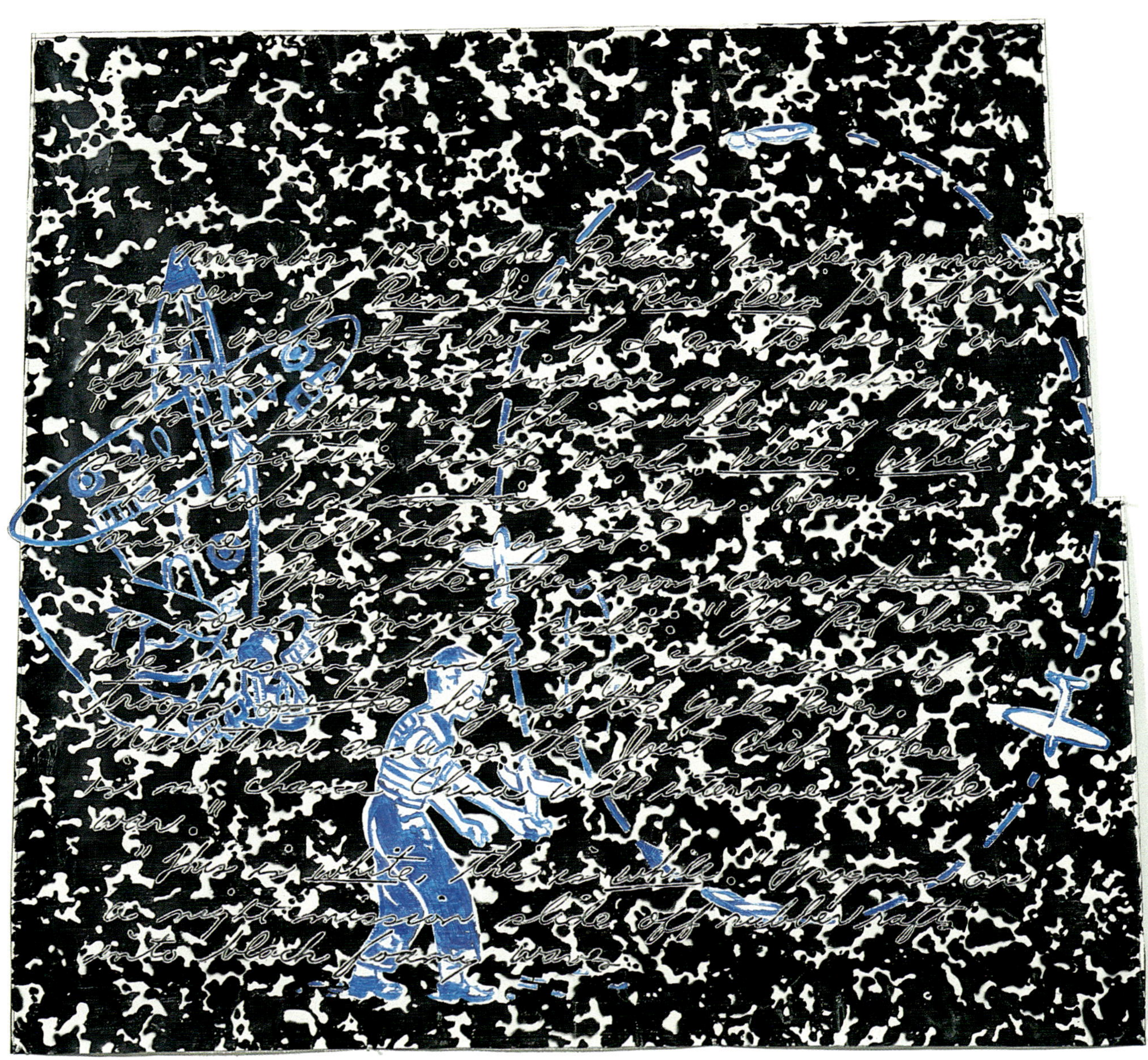

Vernon Fisher
Boy Throwing Airplane   1983
acrylic on laminated paper
74½ x 80
Courtesy Barbara Gladstone
Gallery, New York

Vernon Fisher
Boy Throwing Airplane

November 1950. The palace has been running previews of *Run Silent, Run Deep* for the past week, but if I am to see it on Saturday I must improve my reading. "This is *white* and this is *while*," my mother says, pointing to the words. *White. While.* They look so similar how can anyone ever tell them apart?

From the other room comes a voice on the radio. "The Red Chinese are massing hundreds of thousands of troops beyond the Yalu River. MacArthur assures the joint chiefs there is no chance China will intervene in the war."

White. While. Frogmen on a night mission slide off rubber rafts into black foamy waves.

Show and Tell (p. 27) centers around a more formalized learning situation: a blackboard built by the artist occupies the central portion of the work and calls to mind a classroom. The blackboard appears in numerous works by Fisher, often with all sorts of scientific diagrams—images that he has photographed from textbooks which demonstrate how different physical forces operate. In later works, the blackboard is covered with elaborate diagrams and formulas, foolishly implying that life can be explained logically, but in *Show and Tell* its use is more innocent, intended to conjure up memories of youth, school and learning.

The left-hand image of *Show and Tell* relates to the painting's text in a more straightforward way than in most of Fisher's images. The narrative concerns a painfully shy schoolgirl who lacks the nerve to participate during "sharing time," until one day when she stands up in front of the class, shreds a tissue and announces, "See? Snow." The viewer is left wondering whether she has finally gained the courage to speak or is rebelliously mocking the show-and-tell practice with her pert demonstration. The text is etched into an image of grinning fishermen, showing off their catch for all to admire. While in one sense the text parallels the painted image, the ease with which the adults display their achievement contrasts with the youngster's great difficulty, offering the optimistic note that life gets easier as one gets older. Aunt Fritzi, a character from the Nancy comic strip, provides a counterpoint to the larger elements in *Show and Tell*, appearing on the sidelines as a commentator on the scene. Her gesture and glance suggest that she is showing and telling us about the rest of the image. As in all of Fisher's work, it is of course the viewer who must ultimately construct his own story, drawing on personal experience to define the various elements and their relationships to one another.

As we have seen, the paintings and photographs of these three artists are decidely narrative in flavor; they reintroduce storytelling in art with a variety of formal inventions that reinforce the power of their observations about childhood. In Fischl's paintings on paper, the overlaid glassine sheets partially obscure the rear images, a format that reveals the working process and suggests in physical terms the passage of time. Fisher's incorporation of text shapes the narrative character of his work, which is a unique blend of words, images and three-dimensional objects; the multipanel structure adds a cinematic touch. Simmons, in her photographs, which vary from bright, almost lurid color to muted black-and-white, also probes the past, creating images that are at times painfully clear and at other times maddeningly hazy.

What is it about today's world that prompts these artists—and others—to explore the terrain of early experience? We live in an age when adults are more knowledgeable and more concerned than ever with issues of child development. In the end, this may explain the direct focus on childhood in the works of Fischl, Simmons and Fisher. Only in an age that fully accepts the need to call up the past in order to explain or master the present could artists have abandoned the relatively more symbolic treatment of childhood common to earlier art. And the transition from the hegemony of post-World War II abstraction to a multiplicity of styles which includes figuration only encourages such a development. The years between youth and adulthood afford a distance that invites artistic inventiveness. What has emerged from the investigations of these artists into the experience of growing up is a series of unforgettable images and art that demonstrates the insight and talent of mature adults.

Footnotes

1. Mary Frances Durantini, *The Child in Seventeenth-Century Dutch Painting* (Ann Arbor, Michigan: UMI Research Press, 1983), p. 3. Jacques Stella's *Les jeux et plaisirs de l'enfance*, a set of fifty-two engraved scenes illustrating children's games and published in 1657, is also not as directly about children as would first appear. The "children" are naked putti, physically indistinguishable from one another, and the accompanying verses strongly hint at adult behavior.
2. Durantini, *The Child in Seventeenth-Century Dutch Painting*, p. 183.
3. Carol Duncan, "Happy Mothers and Other New Ideas in French Art," *The Art Bulletin*, vol. 55 (December 1973), pp. 574-577.
4. O.K. Werckmeister, "The Issue of Childhood in the Art of Paul Klee," *Arts Magazine*, vol. 52 (September 1977), p. 138.
5. Charles Baudelaire, "The Painter of Modern Life," in *The Painter of Modern Life and Other Essays*, translated and edited by Jonathan Mayne (reprint, New York: Da Capo Press, 1986), p. 8.
6. "Fischl Talks," *Vanity Fair*, vol. 47 (May 1984), p. 72.
7. Fischl takes this idea to its logical extreme in *Year of the Drowned Dog* (1983), a print consisting of six opaque panels which the viewer is free to rearrange.
8. Conversation with the artist, January 1986.
9. Conversation with the artist, September 1986.
10. "Interview: Vernon Fisher and Kathy Halbreich, September 1982," *Mediums of Language: Vernon Fisher, Myrel Chernick, Paul Sharits*, exhibition catalogue (Cambridge, Massachusetts: Hayden Gallery, Massachusetts Institute of Technology, 1982), n.p.

Checklist

Dimensions are in inches;
height precedes width.

1. **Eric Fischl**
   Mother and Son at Table   1978
   oil on glassine (5 panels)
   72 x 121
   Collection the artist
   Courtesy Mary Boone Gallery,
   New York
   p. 11

2. **Eric Fischl**
   Critics   1979
   oil on glassine (5 panels)
   72 x 121
   Collection the artist
   Courtesy Mary Boone Gallery,
   New York
   p. 4

3. **Eric Fischl**
   Horse and Rider   1979
   oil on glassine (4 panels)
   60 x 79
   Collection the artist
   Courtesy Mary Boone Gallery,
   New York
   p. 12

4. **Eric Fischl**
   Life Saver/Life Preserver   1979
   oil on glassine (3 panels)
   65 x 84
   Collection the artist
   Courtesy Mary Boone Gallery,
   New York

5. **Eric Fischl**
   Birthday Party   1980
   oil on glassine (4 panels)
   69 x 76
   Collection the artist
   Courtesy Mary Boone Gallery,
   New York
   p. 11

6. **Eric Fischl**
   *Saturday Night
   (the Aftermath Bath)*   1980
   oil on glassine (4 panels)
   72 x 84
   Collection the artist
   Courtesy Mary Boone Gallery,
   New York

7. **Eric Fischl**
   Best Western (first version)   1983
   oil on canvas (3 panels)
   84 x 80
   Collection the artist
   Courtesy Mary Boone Gallery,
   New York
   p. 13

8. **Vernon Fisher**
   Tarzan's Adventure   1980
   acrylic on wood, graphite, plexiglas,
   paint on wall (3 units)
   48 x 174
   Collection Laura L. Carpenter
   pp. 21 (detail), 23

9. **Vernon Fisher**
   Show and Tell   1981
   photograph, oil on wood, blackboard
   60 x 174
   Courtesy Barbara Gladstone Gallery,
   New York
   p. 27

10. **Vernon Fisher**
    Boy Throwing Airplane   1983
    acrylic on laminated paper
    74½ x 80
    Courtesy Barbara Gladstone Gallery,
    New York
    p. 28

11. **Vernon Fisher**
    When I Was a Kid   1983
    eggs, plaster, wood, fan, acrylic
    on paper, metal
    60½ x 131 x 4¾
    35 x 15 x 15 (fan on stool)
    Collection Arthur and Carol Goldberg,
    New York
    p. 25

12. **Laurie Simmons**
Untitled   1976
black-and-white photograph
44½ x 29½
Courtesy Metro Pictures, New York

13. **Laurie Simmons**
Untitled   1976
black-and-white photograph
44½ x 29½
Courtesy Metro Pictures, New York

14. **Laurie Simmons**
Untitled   1976
black-and-white photograph
44½ x 29½
Courtesy Metro Pictures,
New York

15. **Laurie Simmons**
*New Bathroom/Woman
Standing*   1978/87
color photograph
40 x 50
Courtesy Metro Pictures,
New York
p. 15

16. **Laurie Simmons**
Woman/Purple Dress/Kitchen
1978/87
color photograph
40 x 50
Collection Walker Art Center
Jerome Foundation Purchase Fund
For Emerging Artists
p. 15

17. **Laurie Simmons**
Woman/Reading   1978/87
color photograph
40 x 50
Courtesy Metro Pictures,
New York

18-25. **Laurie Simmons**
Untitled (from Family Collision
series)   1981
8 black-and-white photographs
16 x 20 each
Collection Carroll Dunham
p. 16

26. **Laurie Simmons**
Untitled (from Family Collision
series)   1981
color photograph
27½ x 39
Courtesy Metro Pictures,
New York

27. **Laurie Simmons**
Untitled   1981
1 black-and-white and 1 color
photograph
30 x 40 each
Collection Lewis Baskerville

28-29. **Laurie Simmons**
Untitled (from Ventriloquism
series)   1987
2 color photographs
20 x 24 each
Courtesy Metro Pictures,
New York
p. 18

Eric Fischl

Born 1948,
New York City.
B.F.A., 1972,
California Institute of
the Arts, Valencia.
Lives in New York.

One-Artist Exhibitions
1975
· *Bridge/Shield/Shelter*, Dalhousie Art Gallery, Halifax, Novia Scotia ♣
1976
· Studio, Halifax, Nova Scotia
· Galerie B., Montreal
1978
· Galerie B., Montreal
1980
· Edward Thorp Gallery, New York
· Davis Art Gallery, University of Akron, Ohio
1981
· Sable-Castelli Gallery, Toronto
· Edward Thorp Gallery, New York
1982
· University of Colorado Art Gallery, Boulder
· Edward Thorp Gallery, New York
· Sable-Castelli Gallery, Toronto
1983
· Sir George Williams Art Gallery, Montreal
· Saidye Bronfman Centre, Montreal ♣
· Larry Gagosian Gallery, Los Angeles
· Galleria Mario Diacono, Rome
· Multiples Inc., New York
1984
· Mary Boone Gallery, New York
1985
· *Eric Fischl: Paintings*, Mendel Art Gallery, Saskatoon, Saskatchewan (traveled to the Stedelijk Van Abbemuseum, Eindhoven, The Netherlands; Kunsthalle Basel, Switzerland; Institute of Contemporary Arts, London; Art Gallery of Ontario, Toronto; Museum of Contemporary Art, Chicago; Whitney Museum of American Art, New York) ♣
· *The Works on Glassine 1979-80*, Mario Diacono Gallery, Boston ♣
· Sable-Castelli Gallery, Toronto

1986
· Mary Boone Gallery, New York
· Larry Gagosian Gallery, Los Angeles
· Daniel Weinberg Gallery, Los Angeles
· *Eric Fischl: Scenes Before the Eyes*, University Art Museum, California State University, Long Beach (traveled to the University Art Museum, University of Caifornia, Berkeley; Contemporary Arts Center, Honolulu; The Baltimore Museum of Art; The St. Louis Art Museum) ♣
1987
· Mary Boone Gallery, New York

Selected Group Exhibitions
1976
· *Seventeen Artists: A Protean View*, Vancouver Art Gallery, British Columbia ♣
1978
· *Neun Kanadisches Künstlers*, Kunsthalle Basel, Switzerland ♣
1981
· *Real Life Magazine*, Nigel Greenwood Gallery, London
· *Large Format Drawings*, Barbara Toll Fine Arts, New York
1982
· *Critical Perspectives*, P.S. 1, Long Island City, New York
· *Focus on the Figure: Twenty Years*, Whitney Museum of American Art, New York
· *The Expressionist Image: From Pollock to Today*, Sidney Janis Gallery, New York
· Edward Thorp Gallery, New York
· *Figures of Mystery*, The Queens Museum, Flushing, New York
· *New Figuration in America*, Milwaukee Art Museum ♣
· *Drawing: An Exploration of Line*, The Decker Gallery, Maryland Institute, College of Art, Baltimore
1983
· *Reallegory*, Chrysler Museum, Norfolk, Virginia
· *1983 Biennial Exhibition*, Whitney Museum of American Art, New York ♣
· *Paintings*, Mary Boone Gallery, New York

♣ Exhibition catalogue

- *Back to the USA*, Kunstmuseum Luzern, Lucerne, Switzerland (traveled to Rheinisches Landesmuseum, Bonn; Württembergischer Kunstverein, Stuttgart) ♣
- *Tendencias en Nueva York*, Palacio de Cristal, Madrid ♣
- *American Still Life*, Contemporary Arts Museum, Houston (traveled to the Albright-Knox Art Gallery, Buffalo; Columbus Museum of Art, Ohio) ♣
    1984
- *Modern Expressionists*, Sidney Janis Gallery, New York
- *New Painting*, Krannert Art Museum, University of Illinois, Champaign ♣
- *Painting and Sculpture Today*, Indianapolis Museum of Art ♣
- *New Painting*, Musée d'Art Contemporain, Montreal
- *Seventh Dalhousie Drawing Show*, Dalhousie Art Gallery, Halifax, Novia Scotia ♣
- *An International Survey of Painting and Sculpture*, The Museum of Modern Art, New York ♣
- *XLI Biennale di Venezia*, Venice ♣
- *The Human Condition: SFMMA Biennial III*, San Francisco Museum of Modern Art ♣
- *Aspekte Amerikanischer Kunst der Gegenwart*, Neue Galerie-Sammlung Ludwig, Aachen, West Germany
- *Drawings After Photography*, Allen Memorial Art Museum, Oberlin College, Ohio
- *Content*, Hirshhorn Museum and Sculpture Garden, Smithsonian Institution, Washington, D.C. ♣
    1985
- *1985 Biennial Exhibition*, Whitney Museum of American Art, New York ♣
- *XIII Biennale de Paris*, Paris
- *1985 Carnegie International*, Museum of Art, Carnegie Institute, Pittsburgh ♣
    1986
- *An American Renaissance: Painting and Sculpture Since 1940*, Museum of Art, Fort Lauderdale, Florida ♣
- *Biennial of Sydney*, Sydney, Australia
- *Europa/Amerika*, Museum Ludwig, Cologne ♣

- *Individuals: A Selected History of Contemporary Art, 1945-1986*, Museum of Contemporary Art, Los Angeles ♣
    1987
- *State of the Art*, Institute of Contemporary Arts, London ♣
- *Avant-Garde in the Eighties*, Los Angeles County Museum of Art ♣

Vernon Fisher

Born 1943, Fort Worth.
B.A., 1967,
Hardin-Simmons University,
Abilene, Texas.
M.F.A., 1969,
University of Illinois,
Champaign-Urbana.
Lives in Fort Worth.

One-Artist Exhibitions

1973
· *Wall Fragments and Notebooks*, Smither Gallery, Dallas
· *123456 Vernon Fisher*, Tyler Museum of Art, Tyler, Texas ♣

1975
· Delahunty Gallery, Dallas
· Tyler Museum of Art, Tyler, Texas ♣

1976
· William Sawyer Gallery, San Francisco
· *Drawings 1974-76*, The University of Texas at Dallas

1977
· *Paintings, Drawings and Photographs*, Delahunty Gallery, Dallas

1979
· *Vernon Fisher: New Works*, Delahunty Gallery, Dallas

1980
· Galerie Denise René/Hans Mayer, Düsseldorf

1981
· *Vernon Fisher: Story Paintings and Drawings*, Contemporary Arts Museum, Houston ♣
· *Breaking the Code*, Franklin Furnace, New York
· *Vernon Fisher New Work*, Barbara Gladstone Gallery, New York

1982
· Delahunty Gallery, Dallas
· Galerie T'Venster, Rotterdam ♣

1983
· Barbara Gladstone Gallery, New York
· Madison Art Center, Madison, Wisconsin

1984
· Barbara Gladstone Gallery, New York

1985
· Butler Gallery, Houston

1986
· Asher-Faure Gallery, Los Angeles

1987
· *Building Our House*, Barbara Gladstone Gallery, New York

Selected Group Exhibitions

1970
· *Project South/Southwest*, Fort Worth Art Center ♣

1972
· *Exhibition of Ten Texas Painters*, Art Museum of South Texas, Corpus Christi

1975
· *Exchange DFW/SFO*, Fort Worth Art Museum (traveled to the San Francisco Museum of Modern Art)

1977
· *American Narrative/Story Art 1967-1977*, Contemporary Arts Museum, Houston

1978
· *Corsicana Panorama*, Warehouse Living Arts Center, Corsicana, Texas
· *Chandelier*, Delahunty Gallery, Dallas
· *Texas in Chicago: Green, Fisher, Surls, Wade*, Marianne Deson Gallery, Chicago
· *Art of Texas*, The Renaissance Society at the University of Chicago

1979
· *Fire! An Exhibition of 100 Texas Artists*, Contemporary Arts Museum, Houston
· *Paper Works: An Exhibition of Texas Artists*, Witte Museum, San Antonio ♣

1980
· *Response*, Tyler Museum of Art, Tyler, Texas ♣
· *Investigations: Probe * Structure * Analysis*, The New Museum of Contemporary Art, New York ♣

1981
· *19 Emergent Americans: 1981 Exxon National Exhibition*, The Solomon R. Guggenheim Museum, New York ♣
· *1981 Biennial Exhibition*, Whitney Museum of American Art, New York ♣
· *Directions 1981*, Hirshhorn Museum and Sculpture Garden, Smithsonian Institution, Washington, D.C. ♣
· *Words and Images*, The Renaissance Society at the University of Chicago
· *A Texas Group Show*, Charles Cowles Gallery, New York
· *Drawings*, Glen Hanson Gallery, Minneapolis
· *The Southern Voice: Terry Allen, Vernon Fisher, Ed McGowin*, Fort Worth Art Museum ♣

♣ Exhibition catalogue

1982
- *Currents: A New Mannerism, Part I,* University of South Florida, Tampa ♣
- *Mediums of Language: Vernon Fisher, Myrel Chernick, Paul Sharits,* Hayden Gallery, Massachusetts Institute of Technology, Cambridge ♣
- *Still Modern After All These Years,* Chrysler Museum, Norfolk, Virginia
- *The Americans: The Collage,* Contemporary Arts Museum, Houston ♣
- *Painting and Sculpture Today 1982,* Indianapolis Museum of Art ♣
- *Fifth India Triennial,* New Delhi, India
- *Stroke/Line/Figure,* Gimpel Fils, London

1983
- *The Comic Art Show,* Whitney Museum of American Art, Downtown Branch, New York
- *Fact and Fiction,* Aspen Center for the Visual Arts, Colorado
- *Language, Drama, Source and Vision,* The New Museum of Contemporary Art, New York
- *Comment.,* Long Beach Museum of Art, Long Beach, California ♣
- *Second Western States Exhibition—The 38th Corcoran Biennial Exhibition of American Paintings,* The Corcoran Gallery of Art, Washington, D.C. (traveled to the Lakeview Museum of Arts and Sciences, Peoria, Illinois; Scotsdale Center for the Arts, Scotsdale, Arizona; Alberquerque Museum, New Mexico; Long Beach Museum of Art, Long Beach, California; San Francisco Museum of Modern Art) ♣

1984
- *Southern Fictions,* Contemporary Arts Museum, Houston ♣
- *El Arte Narrativo,* Museo Rufino Tamayo, Mexico City ♣
- *Content: A Contemporary Focus 1974-1984,* Hirshhorn Museum and Sculpture Garden, Smithsonian Institution, Washington, D.C. ♣
- *New American Painting,* Archer M. Huntington Art Gallery, University of Texas, Austin ♣
- *Words = Pictures,* The Bronx Museum, Bronx, New York
- *Fragment/Fragmentary/Fragmentation,* The New Britain Museum of American Art, New Britain, Connecticut
- *The Shadow of the Bomb,* Mt. Holyoke College Gallery, South Hadley, Massachusetts

1985
- Barbara Toll Fine Arts, New York
- *Comic Relief,* Barry Whistler Gallery, Dallas

1986
- *Five Texas Artists,* McIntosh/Drysdale Gallery, Washington, D.C.
- *Public and Private: American Prints Today: The 24th National Print Exhibition,* The Brooklyn Museum, New York (traveled to the Flint Institute of Arts, Michigan; Museum of Art, Rhode Island School of Design, Providence; Museum of Art, Carnegie Institute, Pittsburgh; Walker Art Center, Minneapolis) ♣
- *New Orleans Triennial: The Centennial Exhibition,* New Orleans Museum of Art
- *Seventy-Fifth American Exhibition,* The Art Institute of Chicago
- *The Texas Landscape 1900-1986,* The Museum of Fine Arts, Houston
- *Wall Works,* John Weber Gallery, New York
- *Memento Mori,* Centro Culturale de Arte Contemporaneo, Mexico City ♣
- *Text & Image: The Wording of American Art,* Holly Solomon Gallery, New York
- *A Cabinet of Drawings,* Gimpel Fils, London

Laurie Simmons

Born 1949,
Far Rockaway, New York.
B.F.A., 1971,
Tyler School of Art,
Philadelphia.
Lives in New York.

One-Artist Exhibitions

1979
- Artists Space, New York
- P.S. 1, Long Island, New York
- University of Rhode Island, Kingston

1981
- Diane Brown Gallery, Washington, D.C.
- Metro Pictures, New York

1983
- Metro Pictures, New York
- CEPA Gallery, Buffalo

1984
- Galerie Tanjua Grunert, Stuttgart
- International With Monument Gallery, New York

1985
- Weatherspoon Art Gallery, University of North Carolina, Greensboro
- *Actual Photos* (collaboration with Allan McCollum), Nature Morte Gallery, New York (traveled to Rhona Hoffman Gallery, Chicago; Heath Gallery, Atlanta; Texas Gallery, Houston; Kuhlenschmidt/Simon Gallery, Los Angeles)
- Tyler School of Art, Philadelphia
- Josh Baer Gallery, New York

Selected Group Exhibitions

1979
- *Re: Figuration*, Max Protetch Gallery, New York

1980
- *Invented Images*, University Art Museum, University of California, Santa Barbara, California (traveled to Portland Art Museum, Oregon; Mary Porter Sesnon Art Gallery, University of California, Santa Cruz) ♣
- *Presences: The Figure and Man-made Environments*, Freedman Gallery, Albright College, Reading, Pennsylvania ♣
- *Model Photography*, CEPA Gallery, Buffalo
- *Opening Group Exhibition*, Metro Pictures, New York
- *Image Fabriquée*, Galerie Viviane Esders, Paris

1981
- *Pictures and Promises*, The Kitchen, New York
- *Fabricated to Be Photographed*, Fine Arts Gallery, Wright State University, Dayton, Ohio ♣
- *Staged Shots*, Delahunty Gallery, New York
- *Eight Contemporary Photographers*, University Galleries, University of South Florida, Tampa
- *Carey/Dwyer/Simmons/Skoglund*, Texas Gallery, Houston
- *Color Photography: 5 New Views*, Marlborough Gallery, New York
- *Love Is Blind*, Castelli Graphics, New York
- *Photo*, Metro Pictures, New York
- *Body Language: Figurative Aspects of Recent Art*, Hayden Gallery, Massachusetts Institute of Technology, Cambridge (traveled to Fort Worth Art Museum; University Galleries, University of South Florida, Tampa; Contemporary Arts Center, Cincinnati) ♣
- *Erweiterte Fotografie*, Wiener Internationale Bienale, Vienna ♣
- *Figures: Forms and Expressions*, Albright-Knox Art Gallery, Buffalo ♣
- *35 Artists Return to Artists Space*, Artists Space, New York

1982
- *New New York*, Florida State University Fine Arts Gallery, Tallahassee (traveled to the Metropolitan Museum and Art Center, Coral Gables, Florida) ♣
- *Beyond Photography: The Fabricated Image*, Delahunty Gallery, New York
- *The Image Scavengers*, Institute of Contemporary Art, University of Pennsylvania, Philadelphia ♣

1983
- *Images Fabriquées*, Musée National d'Art Moderne, Centre Georges Pompidou, Paris (traveled to the Musée des Beaux-Arts, Nantes; Musée d'Art Actuel, Hasselt, Belgium) ♣
- *Three-Dimensional Photography*, Castelli Graphics, New York
- *Figurative Contexts*, Turman Gallery, Indiana State University, Terre Haute
- *In Plato's Cave*, Marlborough Gallery, New York ♣
- *Subjective Vision*, The High Museum of Art, Atlanta ♣

♣ Exhibition catalogue

1984

- Metro Pictures, New York
- *Masking/Unmasking: Aspects of Post-Modernist Photography*, The Friends of Photography, Carmel, California
- *Family of Man*, P.S. 1, Long Island City, New York
- *Still Life with Transaction*, International With Monument Gallery, New York
- *Visions of Childhood: A Contemporary Iconography*, Whitney Museum of American Art, Downtown Branch, New York
- *Painting and Sculpture Today*, Indianapolis Museum of Art ♣
- *A Decade of New Art*, Artists Space, New York ♣
- *The International Show*, Baskerville + Watson Gallery, New York
- *Women of Influence*, Amerika Haus Berlin, West Berlin ♣
- *Con Rumore*, Rotterdamse Kunststichting, Rotterdam ♣
- *Between Here and Nowhere*, Riverside Studios, London ♣
- *Marcus Leatherdale, Robert Mapplethorpe, Laurie Simmons—Still Life Photographs*, Jason McCoy Inc., New York

1985

- International With Monument Gallery, New York
- *Louise Lawler, Laurie Simmons, James Welling*, Metro Pictures, New York
- *1985 Biennial Exhibition*, Whitney Museum of American Art, New York ♣
- *XVIII Bienal Internacional de São Paulo*, São Paulo
- *The Parodic Power of Popular Imagery*, Queensboro Community College Gallery, Bayside, New York (traveled to the Freedman Gallery, Albright College, Reading, Pennsylvania)
- *Swimmers*, Pace/MacGill Gallery, New York
- *Illuminating Color: Four Approaches in Contemporary Painting and Photography*, Pratt Institute Gallery, Brooklyn, New York
- *Big Portraits*, Jeffrey Hoffeld Gallery, New York

- *New York Now: Correspondences*, Laforet Museum, Tokyo (traveled to the Tochigi Prefectural Museum of Fine Arts, Tochigi; Tazaki Hall Media, Kobe, Japan)

1986

- Metro Pictures, New York
- *The Real Big Picture*, The Queens Museum, Flushing, New York
- *Biennial of Sydney*, Sydney, Australia
- *Photographic Fiction*, Whitney Museum of American Art, Fairfield County, Stamford, Connecticut ♣
- *Last Dance: Glamour, Death, Entertainment*, Palladium, New York
- Metro Pictures, New York
- *Remembrances of Things Past*, Long Beach Museum of Art, Long Beach, California ♣

1987

- International With Monument Gallery, New York

Lenders to the Exhibition

Lewis Baskerville
Laura L. Carpenter
Carroll Dunham
Eric Fischl
Barbara Gladstone Gallery
Carol and Arthur Goldberg
Metro Pictures

Acknowledgments

Thanks are due the many individuals who have assisted with the organization of this exhibition. As always, the staff at Walker, in particular my assistant Brian Hassett and curatorial intern Jennifer Wells, were especially helpful. My colleagues Elizabeth Armstrong, Associate Curator, Walker Art Center, and Lynne Ambrosini, Assistant Curator of Painting, Minneapolis Institute of Arts, kindly provided counsel on the catalogue; I am also in debt to Sheila Schwartz, who edited the catalogue. In addition, the good offices of Western Publishing Company, Inc., Racine, Wisconsin are acknowleged for allowing us to make reference to their Little Golden Books in the catalogue design.

The cooperation of colleagues Sarah Rogers-Lafferty and Dennis Barrie, Contemporary Arts Center, Cincinnati; Ann Shengold, Knight Gallery/Spirit Square Center for the Arts; and Janet Kardon and Judith Tannenbaum, Institute of Contemporary Art, Philadelphia, whose institutions will also host the exhibition, has also been most welcome.

The artists' dealers and their associates, Mary Boone, Ron Warren, Barbara Gladstone, Janelle Reiring and Helene Winer as well as Eric Fischl's assistant, Stacy Milgram, kindly complied with numerous requests and assisted at times in obtaining loans. I would also like to thank the lenders, whose generosity truly made the exhibition possible. Finally, the support of the artists themselves is gratefully acknowleged. It has been a privilege to work with them.

Marge Goldwater

Reproduction Credits

Geoffrey Clements,
courtesy Paula Cooper Gallery
p. 7 (middle)

Steve Dennie
pp. 25, 28

Courtesy Barbara Gladstone Gallery
p. 27

Mates and Katz
p.7 (above)

Eric Pollitzer
p. 8

Laurie Simmons
pp. 15-18

Walker Art Center
pp. 7 (below), 21, 23

Zindman/Fremont,
courtesy Mary Boone Gallery
pp. 4, 9, 11-13